The · Life Cycle · Series

The Life Cycle of a

SHARK

John Crossingham & Bobbie Kalman
♣ Crabtree Publishing Company

www.crabtreebooks.com

The Life Cycle Series

A Bobbie Kalman Book

Dedicated by Samantha Crabtree
To Gage and Chase—wishing you a lifetime full of great adventures

Editor-in-Chief
Bobbie Kalman

Writing team
John Crossingham
Bobbie Kalman

Substantive editor
Kathryn Smithyman

Project editor
Molly Aloian

Editors
Kelley MacAulay
Reagan Miller

Design
Margaret Amy Salter
Samantha Crabtree (cover)

Production coordinator
Heather Fitzpatrick

Photo research
Crystal Foxton

Consultant
Patricia Loesche, Ph.D., Animal Behavior Program,
Department of Psychology, University of Washington

Illustrations
Barbara Bedell: back cover, pages 6, 7, 9 (right), 10, 11 (top), 15
Bonna Rouse: pages 11 (bottom left and right), 13, 14
Margaret Amy Salter: page 9 (left)

Photographs
iStockphoto.com: Paul Johnson: pages 18-19
©Francis Abbott/naturepl.com: page 12
Jeff Rotman/Photo Researchers, Inc.: page 28
SeaPics.com: ©Mark Conlin: page 20; ©Howard Hall: page 22;
    ©Jeff Jaskolski: pages 26-27; ©Scott Michael: page 21;
    ©Doug Perrine: pages 9, 15, 23; ©Andre Seale: page 16;
    ©Jeremy Stafford-Deitsch: page 17; ©Ron & Valerie Taylor: page 29;
    ©Masa Ushioda: page 24
Other images by Corel and Digital Stock

Crabtree Publishing Company

www.crabtreebooks.com   1-800-387-7650

Copyright © **2006 CRABTREE PUBLISHING COMPANY.**
All rights reserved. No part of this publication may be
reproduced, stored in a retrieval system or be transmitted in
any form or by any means, electronic, mechanical, photocopying,
recording, or otherwise, without the prior written permission
of Crabtree Publishing Company. In Canada: We acknowledge
the financial support of the Government of Canada through
the Book Publishing Industry Development Program (BPIDP)
for our publishing activities.

Cataloging-in-Publication Data
Crossingham, John.
  The life cycle of a shark / John Crossingham & Bobbie Kalman.
     p. cm. -- (The life cycle series)
  Includes index.
  ISBN-13: 978-0-7787-0669-4 (rlb)
  ISBN-10: 0-7787-0669-9 (rlb)
  ISBN-13: 978-0-7787-0699-1 (pbk)
  ISBN-10: 0-7787-0699-0 (pbk)
  1. Sharks--Life cycles--Juvenile literature. I. Title.
  QL638.9.C767 2005
  597.3--dc22
                                                    2005020744
                                                    LC

**Published in
the United States**
PMB16A
350 Fifth Ave.
Suite 3308
New York, NY
10118

**Published
in Canada**
616 Welland Ave.,
St. Catharines, Ontario
Canada
L2M 5V6

**Published in the
United Kingdom**
73 Lime Walk
Headington
Oxford
OX3 7AD
United Kingdom

**Published
in Australia**
386 Mt. Alexander Rd.,
Ascot Vale (Melbourne)
VIC 3032

Contents

What is a shark?

Sharks are fish. Like all fish, sharks live in water. Sharks have body parts called **gills** for breathing under water. Sharks are **cold-blooded** animals. The body temperatures of cold-blooded animals change as the temperatures of their surroundings change.

Cartilaginous fish

Sharks are **vertebrates**. Vertebrates are animals with backbones. Sharks do not have hard bones, however. They are **cartilaginous** fish. The skeletons of cartilaginous fish are made of **cartilage**. Cartilage is a tough, **flexible**, or bendable, material. It is lighter than bone. Having flexible skeletons helps sharks swim quickly through water.

Sharks have been living on Earth for millions of years.
The first sharks lived on Earth before dinosaurs did.
This shark is a great white shark.

4

Salt water

Sharks live in oceans. Oceans contain salt water. Most sharks must live in salt water to stay alive. Only a few **species**, or types, of sharks are able to spend time in fresh water. Fresh water does not contain salt. Bull sharks can stay in fresh water, but only for a short time. They must then return to salt water.

*Many sharks, including this reef shark, live in **coral reefs**. Coral reefs are large rocklike structures found in the shallow waters of **tropical oceans**.*

Ocean homes

Sharks live in all the world's oceans, except perhaps the coldest parts of the Southern Ocean, near Antarctica. Some species of sharks live in icy **polar oceans**, some live in **temperate oceans**, and others live in warm tropical oceans. Certain sharks live only in shallow parts of oceans. Others live only in deep water. A few species of sharks move between deep and shallow water.

This nurse shark lives near the ocean floor in tropical oceans. Some nurse sharks live in water that is up to 70 feet (21 m) deep.

5

So many sharks!

There are about 450 known species of sharks. All sharks have the same main body parts, but each species of shark looks different.

Some sharks, such as whale sharks, are large. Other sharks, such as spiny dogfish sharks, are small.

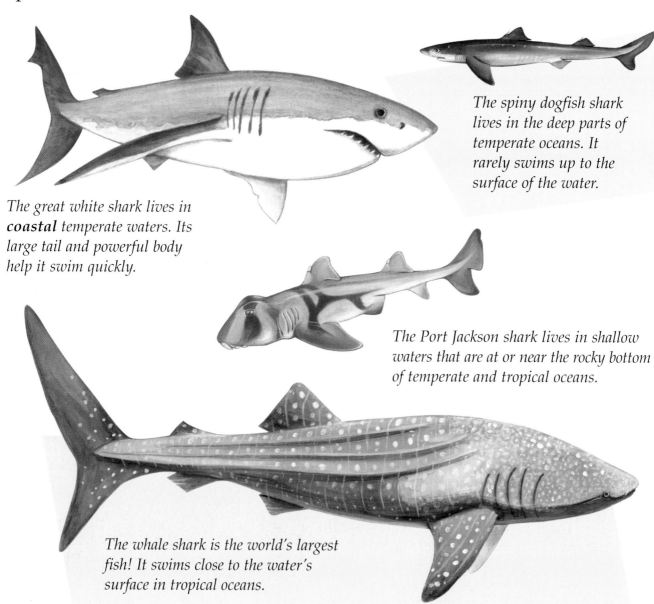

The spiny dogfish shark lives in the deep parts of temperate oceans. It rarely swims up to the surface of the water.

*The great white shark lives in **coastal** temperate waters. Its large tail and powerful body help it swim quickly.*

The Port Jackson shark lives in shallow waters that are at or near the rocky bottom of temperate and tropical oceans.

The whale shark is the world's largest fish! It swims close to the water's surface in tropical oceans.

The hammerhead
shark lives throughout
temperate oceans. It
has an eye on each side
of its wide head.

The sawshark lives on the mud, sand,
or gravel at the bottom of temperate
and tropical oceans.

The tiger shark lives
in tropical waters.
It has stripes on its body,
just as a tiger has.

The angel shark often buries
itself in the sand or mud at
the bottom of temperate or
tropical oceans.

7

A shark's body

Most sharks have **streamlined**, or sleek, bodies. Having streamlined bodies allows sharks to swim through water easily. A few shark species are called **bottom dwellers**.

Bottom dwellers are sharks that swim along the bottom of oceans and often rest on ocean floors. Most bottom-dwelling sharks have wide, flat bodies.

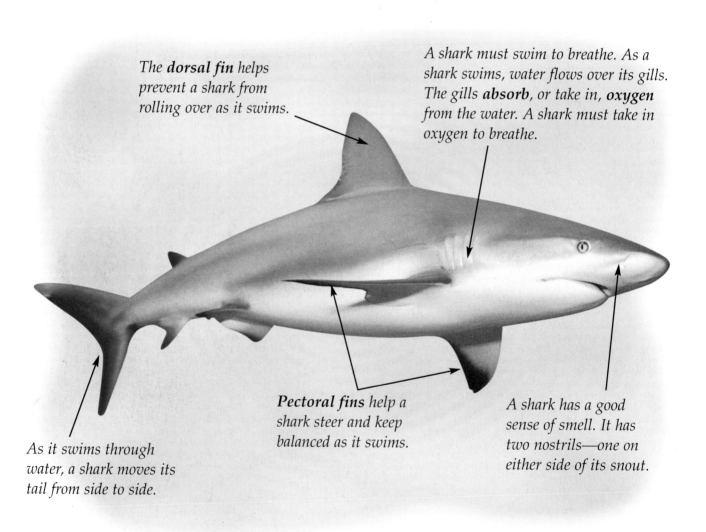

The **dorsal fin** helps prevent a shark from rolling over as it swims.

A shark must swim to breathe. As a shark swims, water flows over its gills. The gills **absorb**, or take in, **oxygen** from the water. A shark must take in oxygen to breathe.

As it swims through water, a shark moves its tail from side to side.

Pectoral fins help a shark steer and keep balanced as it swims.

A shark has a good sense of smell. It has two nostrils—one on either side of its snout.

Light in the water

A shark has an **organ** inside its body called a **liver**. Most sharks have large livers. A shark's liver is filled with oil. The oil inside the shark's liver is lighter than the water around the shark's body. Having an oil-filled liver helps the shark swim easily through water.

Feel the moves

A shark has hundreds of tiny, jelly-filled **pores**, or holes, on its face. These pores are called **ampullae of Lorenzini**. They help the shark feel even the slightest movements in water. For example, a shark can feel the movements made by a fish, even when the fish is buried in sand.

Sandpaper skin

A shark's skin is covered with rough, toothlike **denticles**, which are similar to snake scales. A shark's denticles are joined together and form a protective layer over the shark's skin. The denticles are coated in tough **enamel**—the same material that covers your teeth.

When a shark's denticles grow old, they fall off. New denticles grow in to replace the old denticles.

What is a life cycle?

Sharks that live in tropical oceans far from land, such as this mako shark, grow faster than do sharks that live in colder waters.

Every animal goes through a **life cycle**. A life cycle is made up of the **stages**, or changes, which an animal goes through during its life. First, an animal is born or hatches from an egg. The animal then grows and changes until it becomes **mature**, or an adult. As an adult, the animal can **mate**, or join together to make babies.

Life span

An animal's **life span** is not the same as its life cycle. A life span is the length of time an animal is alive. Different sharks have different life spans.

The life spans of large sharks are usually longer than are the life spans of small sharks. Most sharks, including the great white shark, live for about 25 years. The whale shark can live to be 70 years old!

A shark's life cycle

Most sharks begin their life cycles as eggs. An **embryo**, or developing baby, grows inside each egg. A female shark carries the eggs inside her body. She can carry between two and fourteen eggs at a time. When the embryos are ready, they hatch while they are still inside their mother. After the embryos hatch, they **emerge**, or come out, from their mother's body. Newborn sharks are called **pups**. They look like small adult sharks. Pups grow slowly into **juvenile** sharks. Between eight and twelve years old, the juvenile sharks become mature sharks. The mature sharks are then able to make babies of their own.

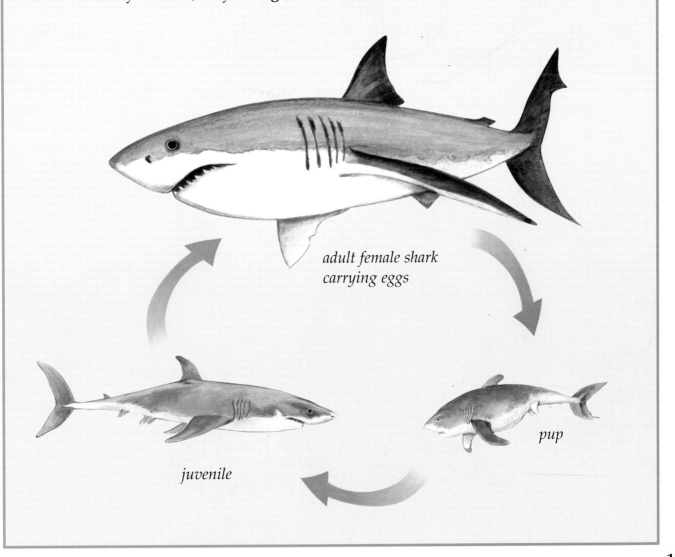

adult female shark carrying eggs

pup

juvenile

Growing inside

A **pregnant** female shark has embryos developing inside her body. The embryos are safe there. Her body provides them with the perfect temperature for growing. Most female sharks are pregnant for about twelve months.

This female nurse shark is pregnant. She will carry the embryos inside her body for eleven to twelve months.

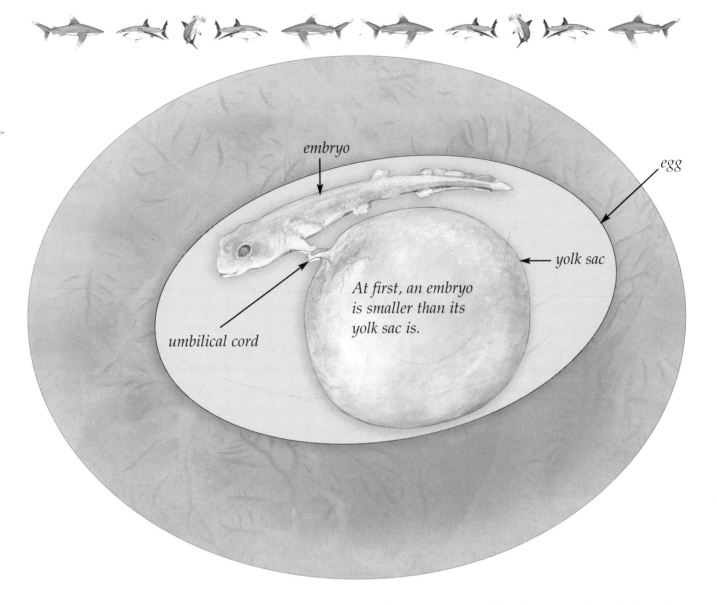

embryo

egg

umbilical cord

yolk sac

At first, an embryo is smaller than its yolk sac is.

Inside the egg

Each embryo develops inside an egg. The egg provides the developing embryo with food, shelter, and oxygen. Oxygen from the mother's body flows in and out of the egg, allowing the embryo to breathe.

The area inside the mother's body that holds the egg is called the **oviduct**. A big **yolk sac** is attached to the embryo by an **umbilical cord**. The yolk sac holds food for the embryo. As the embryo grows, its skin develops denticles and its body becomes bigger.

13

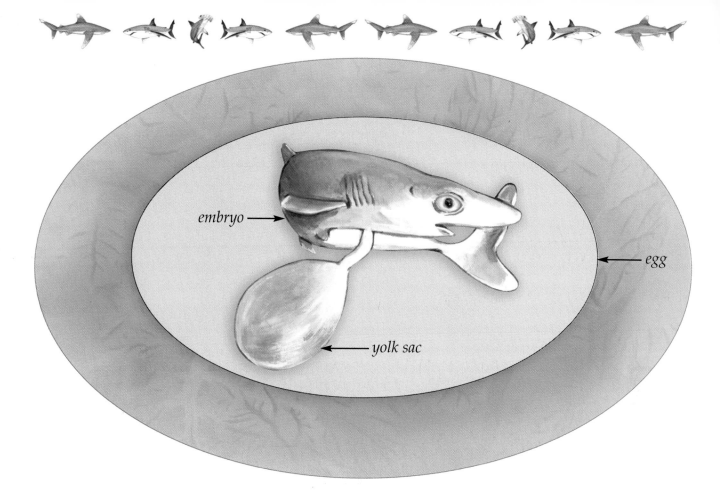

embryo →

← *egg*

← *yolk sac*

Time to hatch!

The growing embryo soon becomes larger than its yolk sac. Eventually, the embryo becomes too large for its egg. It has eaten all the food inside the yolk sac and is now ready to hatch. The embryo twists and turns its body in order to burst out of its egg. It uses its denticles to grip the sides of the egg and to wiggle itself out of it.

To the nursery!
A mother shark can feel when her pups have hatched inside her body and are ready to emerge. She swims to warm, shallow water that has many coral reefs and rocky areas. The place where a female shark gives birth is called a **nursery**.

Tail first

Soon after the pups have hatched from their eggs, they wriggle out of their mother's body and into the water. Most pups come out of their mother's body tail first, although a few species emerge headfirst.

Folded up

The pups of some species, such as hammerhead sharks or sawsharks, have spines, teeth, or oddly shaped heads that stick out. When the pups emerge, these body parts are folded close to their bodies. With the body parts folded into their bodies, the pups can slide out easily from their mothers' bodies.

A newborn pup wiggles wildly in the ocean until its umbilical cord falls off. This newborn tiger shark has just shaken off its umbilical cord.

Young sharks

Mother sharks do not care for their pups after the pups are born. Shark pups are born knowing how to hunt for food and how to hide from **predators**. Predators are animals that hunt other animals for food. The animals that predators hunt are called **prey**.

Newborn pups are prey for adult sharks and other animals, but pups are fairly safe in nurseries. The pups stay safe by hiding among plants and rocks. They hunt for shrimps, small fish, and tiny crabs.

This hammerhead shark pup is searching for its first meal. There is plenty of food in its nursery.

Slow to grow

Although they eat plenty of food, shark pups grow much slower than other fish do. All sharks take several years to become mature, but small sharks often grow faster than large sharks do. While they are young, shark pups are constantly in danger of being eaten by predators.

Leaving the nursery

Older shark pups are often called juveniles. When they are four or five years old, juveniles move to deeper water. There, they feed on large prey, such as squids and big fish. Many juveniles stay in small groups for protection from predators such as adult sharks, dolphins, and barracudas.

This juvenile leopard shark will grow much larger and stronger before it becomes an adult.

Adult life

An adult shark has long, thick teeth and broad, strong denticles. It is big and strong enough to kill and eat large prey. Sharks continue growing throughout their lives. Their bodies never stop growing.

Safe from harm

Adult sharks are also large and strong enough to protect themselves from being eaten. In fact, huge sharks, such as great whites, bull sharks, and tiger sharks, are **apex**, or top, predators. These sharks have no predators because they are too big and powerful to be killed. Adult sharks are **solitary**, which means they live alone. They do not need other sharks to protect them or to help them find food.

Making pups

When it is time to mate, male and female sharks of the same species find one another. Adult female sharks release chemicals called **pheromones** into the water. Male sharks can smell these pheromones from far away. The males follow the scents of the pheromones to find the females. Several males often swim to the same female.

Male sharks that want to mate with a female use their teeth to grab the female by her fins or her back. Female sharks have thick skin that helps protect them from these bites. A female may still receive injuries and scars from the male's bites, however. Eventually, the female mates with the strongest male.

Time to mate

A male shark has two organs called **claspers** that are attached to each of his pelvic fins. The male uses his claspers to place **sperm** inside the female's body. Sperm is a liquid that **fertilizes** the eggs that are inside the female's body. Fertilized eggs have embryos growing inside them.

Small shark species, such these epaulette sharks, are very flexible. A male can wrap its whole tail around the female during mating.

Eggs with a twist

A few species of sharks have slightly different life cycles than the life cycle described on pages 12-15. Some species of female sharks, including horn sharks and swell sharks, do not carry their eggs inside their bodies. Instead, they lay their eggs on the ocean floor. Each female lays a group of about twenty eggs in a sheltered spot.

Anchored eggs

Shark eggs that are laid on the ocean floor often have **casings**, or covers, with spiral ribs or stiff arms called **tendrils**. These shapes help the eggs stay anchored to the ocean floor. If the eggs were not anchored, they could drift into the deeper, colder parts of the ocean. The cold temperatures could harm the embryos inside the eggs. It is also easier for hungry predators to spot drifting eggs.

This horn shark egg case has spiral ribs that anchor the egg to the ocean floor.

22

Who needs an egg?

A few shark species, such as hammerheads, bull sharks, and lemon sharks, do not hatch from eggs at all. The embryos of these sharks grow right inside the bodies of their mothers. Each embryo has a **yolk-sac placenta**, which is attached to the female's body by an umbilical cord. The yolk-sac placenta provides the growing embryo with all the **nutrients** it needs to grow.

Born live

Embryos grow inside the bodies of their mothers for about a year. When the embryos are finished growing, they are **born**. Animals that are born are not inside eggs when they leave the bodies of their mothers. Shark mothers do not feed their pups after they are born. The pups must survive on their own, just as other shark pups must.

On the hunt

Different sharks eat different foods, depending on their size and the way they hunt. Sharks that can swim quickly hunt fast-moving prey, such as dolphins. Some sharks chase down their prey and then bite the prey to kill it. Other fast-swimming sharks use their tails to strike and kill prey before eating it.

Living low

Most bottom-dwelling sharks, such as nurse sharks, hunt crabs, lobsters, squids, and fish that also swim near the bottom of oceans. Many bottom dwellers simply wait on the ocean floor for small fish and other prey to swim by.

This nurse shark used its sharp teeth to catch a fish that was swimming near the ocean floor.

Fast food

Sharks often hunt injured, old, or dying prey. These animals are easy to catch because they cannot fight back or swim away. A shark can hear the wild splashing of an injured animal from miles away. It can smell the blood of a bleeding fish from a great distance and swim right to the animal. Many sharks, such as tiger sharks and blue sharks, also eat **carrion**, or animals that are already dead.

"Toothless" giants

Basking sharks and whale sharks may have teeth, but they do not need them. These sharks are **filter feeders**. To get food, filter feeders swim with their huge mouths open wide and **filter**, or strain, their food from the water. The foods they filter include shrimp, tiny fish, and **plankton**.

This whale shark filters its meal from the water as it swims.

We need sharks

Sharks help keep oceans healthy by eating sick, injured, and dead animals. They also eat other predators, including seals, large fish, and octopuses. Eating these animals helps keep a healthy balance between predator and prey **populations** in oceans.

Population control

By hunting all kinds of fish, octopuses, and seals, sharks keep the populations of these animals from growing too large. For example, if there were no sharks, there may soon be too many other fish. These fish might begin eating too many of another species of animal, which could cause the population of that prey animal to decrease or even to disappear. As a result, there may be an imbalance in predator and prey populations. No one knows exactly what would happen to other animal populations if there were no sharks in the oceans.

26

Dangers to sharks

Many people are afraid of sharks, but sharks face more dangers from people than people do from sharks. Even large apex predators, such as bull sharks and great white sharks, face dangers. Some people hunt sharks for their meat, for their body parts, or for sport. Other people **overfish** in the oceans. Many sharks are also harmed by pollution.

Soup of the day

Sharkfin soup is an expensive and popular food in certain parts of the world. As a result, many sharks are hunted only for their fins. Fishers catch sharks, cut off their fins, and then throw the helpless sharks back into the water. Without their fins, the sharks cannot swim. They quickly sink to the bottom of the ocean and die.

This hammerhead shark does not have fins because a fisher has cut them off.

28

Where's our food?

Fish such as cod, tuna, halibut, and trout are foods that many people enjoy eating. These fish are also prey for many species of sharks. When people overfish and catch too many tuna or halibut, sharks are left without enough food. Many sharks may starve to death as a result.

Garbage in the water

Pollution causes many of the animals on which sharks feed to become sick or to die. Although sharks do not usually suffer from the same sicknesses, they are left without enough food to eat when too many of their prey animals die.

Some sharks die when they are caught in nets meant to catch other fish.

29

Save the sharks!

Large sharks such as lemon sharks and great white sharks are now **endangered** animals. Endangered animals are at risk of disappearing from Earth forever. Sharks need help from people in order to survive.

Protecting sharks

Many governments have passed laws to protect shark populations from overfishing. Some countries have created **marine parks**, which are protected areas in the oceans. These protected areas are safe for all ocean wildlife. Organizations such as **WWF**, or the World Wildlife Fund, are working to raise money and awareness to help protect sharks.

People need to help save great white sharks, such as the one shown above, from being wiped out.

Studying sharks

To learn more about shark behavior, some scientists place **tags** on sharks. A tag is a small plug that has a **transmitter** attached to it. The tag is attached under a shark's dorsal fin. The transmitter sends messages that give scientists information about the routes sharks take to get from place to place and about how far sharks swim. Scientists use the information to learn where sharks swim when they are ready to mate.

Before scientists begin studying sharks in the water, they must learn how to protect themselves and how to avoid shark bites.

Learning more

The biggest challenge sharks face is that people are still afraid of them. Of the more than 400 species of sharks, only 20 species are a threat to people. Many people feel the world would be a safer place without sharks, but sharks are important to ocean life.

Help fight your fear of sharks by learning as much as you can about them. Start by checking out these websites:

- www.oceanofk.org/sharks/sharks
- www.nationalgeographic.com/ngkids/ 0206/shark_cage.html
- www.nationalgeographic.com/kids/ creature_feature/0206/sharks2.html

Glossary

Note: Boldfaced words that are defined in the text may not appear in the glossary.

coastal Ocean waters that are close to land

gills Body parts that fish use to breathe under water

liver An organ that helps break down food and remove wastes from the body

nutrients Substances that living things get from food that are needed for growth and good health

organ A body part, such as the heart or liver, that has an important function

overfish To take too many of one species of animal from oceans

oxygen A gas in air and water that animals must breathe to stay alive

pheromones Chemicals that an animal releases in order to attract other animals of the same species

plankton Tiny plants and animals that live in water

polar ocean A cold ocean that is located at the North Pole or at the South Pole

population The total number of one species of animal in an area

temperate ocean An ocean in a part of the world where the season change

tropical ocean A warm ocean that is located at or near the equator

umbilical cord A cord that connects an embryo to its yolk sac; food and nutrients pass to the embryo through the umbilical cord

Index

1 2 3 4 5 6 7 8 9 0 Printed in the U.S.A. 4 3 2 1 0 9 8 7 6 5